BUSINESS SUITS
TO
COWBOY BOOTS

by Jeannine Dixon Seely

Note for Librarians: A cataloguing record for this book is available from Library and Archives
Canada at www.collectionscanada.ca/amicus/index-e.html
ISBN 1-4120-5989-5

Printed on paper with minimum 30% recycled fibre.
Trafford's print shop runs on "green energy" from solar, wind and other environmentally-friendly
power sources.

TRAFFORD
PUBLISHING™

Offices in Canada, USA, Ireland and UK

This book was published on-demand in cooperation with Trafford Publishing. On-demand
publishing is a unique process and service of making a book available for retail sale to the
public taking advantage of on-demand manufacturing and Internet marketing. On-demand
publishing includes promotions, retail sales, manufacturing, order fulfilment, accounting and
collecting royalties on behalf of the author.

Book sales for North America and international:
Trafford Publishing, 6E–2333 Government St.,
Victoria, BC v8t 4p4 CANADA
phone 250 383 6864 (toll-free 1 888 232 4444)
fax 250 383 6804; email to orders@trafford.com
Book sales in Europe:
Trafford Publishing (uk) Ltd., Enterprise House, Wistaston Road Business Centre,
Wistaston Road, Crewe, Cheshire cw2 7rp United Kingdom
phone 01270 251 396 (local rate 0845 230 9601)
facsimile 01270 254 983; orders.uk@trafford.com
Order online at:
trafford.com/05-0890

10 9 8 7 6 5 4 3 2

CONTENTS

Dedicated to
Dr. Harvey Freed and Judi Freed

ACKNOWLEDGEMENTS

———————————◆————————————————————————◆———————————

Much gratitude to our durable children, James Fox Seely and Timothy Charles Seely who blended in 100% with the back to basics lifestyle.

Love and appreciation to our parents for being so very supportive of our venture.

In memory of Ole and Dee Johnson who taught us city kids so much about country ways.

THANK YOUS

A very special thank you to Maxine Davies, of Everett, Washington for her suggestions, expertise and the encouragement to finish this book, and as always, to my husband, Lee, who has been with me every step of the way in writing our story.

INTRODUCTION

Every now and then, we all run into some unique and wonderful people who become our mentors. Animals included.

Our story touches on some of the special ones that entered ours.

When a once-in-a-lifetime opportunity fell into our laps, we ran with it.

On August 1st, 1969, we owned a spectacular home in Los Angeles, where Lee earned an upper tax bracket wage.

By August 14th-just two weeks later, we lived in a modest ranch house, where the job gave us poverty level pay.

Some logical questions might be, why would we give up all of the luxuries in Los Angeles? How could we leave family and friends? A crazy idea, you might ask?

The answer is simple. Because we wanted to! And the opportunity presented itself at that very moment in our lives.

We invite you to come along with us on thirteen work related moves and a lot of unusual adventures, where you'll meet some rare and down to earth country folks.

The stories regarding our many animal friends might bring a chuckle or even a tear.

Whatever feelings you leave with after reading our story, Lee, our sons, Jim and Tim, and I want to thank you for sharing our adventures of "Business Suits to Cowboy Boots."

BUSINESS SUITS
TO
COWBOY BOOTS

by Jeannine Dixon Seely

Our Day Of Breaking Away

"Bay Fever"

Part 1

OUR DAY OF BREAKING AWAY

Augstust 1969. The war in Vietnam raged, with no end in sight. It was a typical Sunday afternoon at our two story home, perched high on a hill, surrounded by tall walls, spiked gates and security alarms. Lee and I were poolside sipping chilled champagne, and breathing in polluted air. A roaring helicopter in search of evil flew above and siren screams echoed up from the city floor below.

We were unwinding from our hectic week, sharing our dreams of a farm in the country. We'd grow a vegetable garden, gather fresh eggs and our sons would breath clean air. A place far removed from the fast and furious freeways and ever-growing crime in the Los Angeles area. It would be somewhere to escape from the stressful existence we now had, living paycheck to paycheck, just to support our elegant home and lavish lifestyle.

Management of the accounting department at the pharmaceutical firm where Lee worked, had us convinced he was irreplaceable. The generous salary and bonuses reassured us continually. We were dependent on it; we needed it to sustain us.

I was fastened in tight with the P.T.A. and volunteer work was high on my agenda. Our boys, Jim and Tim, who were entering their teens, had sports and Boy Scout activities, which kept us busy every waking hour. There was not a glimmer of light at the top of our whirlwind. We were trapped forever in the secure system of a Los Angeles suburb.

Or were we?

Our lives would change with one phone call. Neighbors Harvey and Judi said they would be right over with a proposal for us to consider. What could it be? The doorbell chimed and they stood there on our threshold, grinning from ear to ear.

Aware of our dreams to find a slower-paced life elsewhere, Judi asked, "How would you like to work on a 1000 acre cattle ranch? My Grandma needs help in northern California. Would you guys be interested in the job?"

My mind raced excitedly. Lee's lips moved to speak but all he could produce was a lame mumble. "Whoa!" I responded, "Run that by again. Especially the part about the 1000 acres!"

They continued, in detail. Judi's widowed Grandmother lived alone twenty miles outside of Red Bluff, California. The job would involve irrigating two pastures, working with 83 head of cattle, three horses, three dogs and sixteen cats. The salary would be a meager $150.00 per month, but the deal included a rent free, furnished house with all utilities paid. Without hesitation we telephoned the lady, who stated, "If you're interested in the job, it's yours, but I need you here in two weeks."

Two weeks!

So little time, so much to do! We made the decision on the spot to cut all ties from the big-city chaos. We were going to transplant our two boys, a Great Dane dog and three Calico cats to this small town 600 miles away, we had never heard of. A house we had never seen. A place where we knew no one. Absolutely no one!

Lee quit his well paying, high pressure job and a 'HOUSE FOR SALE' sign went up on the front lawn. We took four truck and trailer loads of elegant furniture, crystal glassware, excess junk and everyone of Lee's business suits, dress shirts, silk ties and well shined shoes to a flea market and sold every bit of it in two days.

Once word got out we were leaving, our social calendar was jammed full. Friends were in awe, some in near shock, and others downright pessimistic. Remarks like, "You'll be back in six months and then what will you do?" dominated the conversations. Most people were certain we would not survive six months, but the numerous going away brunches and elaborate dinner parties they gave us were well worth their annoying remarks. We tolerated it because WE knew we had made the right choice, we would succeed!

The day of departure arrived along with the realization the house had not sold and we were leaving Los Angeles with $279.00, four rolls of dimes and some loose change in our pockets. We had no credit cards and very little money in the bank to fall back on.

With those frightening facts to consider, we borrowed $300.00 from our stalwart friends, Harvey and Judi.

Our mountain of boxes were hastily packed and distributed among the vehicles. A green, wooden slatted trailer was attached to our bright yellow van, bulging with cherished old family furniture, bunk beds, mattresses and Lee's motorcycle. A 50 pound bag of dog food and a sack of kitty litter was used to wedge the boy's bicycles tightly against some spare tires.

In the final moments, a massive potted date palm tree and an array of worn-out garden hoses were thrown on top of everything and tied down securely with rope.

Lee would drive the van, and I would ride along with him.

Our friend Sonny, a genuine 1960's hippie with a braid down his back, laden in love beads and reeking of Patchouli oil, had offered to drive our '58 Volkswagen Bus, that was named 'Bay Fever'. The boys, the dog and the cats would be his passengers.

At last, it was time to bid farewell to friends and family who'd gathered in and around our circular driveway.

Tears were flowing…We were going on a morning of mixed emotions.

Our day of breaking away!

Sonny Leaves In Search

"House on Silbaugh Ranch"

Part 2

SONNY LEAVES IN SEARCH OF THE TRUTH

The cats hissed and yowled franticly, finally settling down some 300 miles north of Los Angeles. Warbo, the Great Dane went from periodic spurts of vomiting to powerful gas attacks. The boys pestered Sonny, teased one another and pestered the animals. After stopping for fuel and food, Sonny said, "Hey man! This is a real hassle, I can't dig it much longer."

Following lunch, we were back on the road. Within minutes, Sonny pulled over. He'd had it. The nervous cats developed diarrhea and had relieved themselves; as only cats can.

"Hey man, I saw a sign that said San Francisco was only 85 miles. I'm going to hitch a ride and find The Truth from the flower children in Haight Ashbury."

So, I took over as the driver of Bay Fever.

The further north we drove, towns became smaller, vehicles got older, and the manner of dress more casual, with a definite western flair. Hot, tired and anxious to arrive at our destination, we were elated to see a sign, 'Red Bluff, population 7,834'. The directions, given us by Judi's grandmother, led us west of town.

The road was paved the first eight miles, then it turned to dust and tire-destroying pot holes for the next twelve. It seemed like it would never end!

The still, arid air certainly exceeded 100 degrees. Native green grasses in the fields had long been parched brown. Red silt from the road and giant grasshoppers invaded our vehicles. Jim and Tim chanted, "How much longer?", "How much longer?" while darting around the bus grabbing at the hoppers as they jumped from the seats like hot kernels of popped corn.

Bay Fever was a battle zone. It was Lee and I against the dust, and the boys against the bugs.

In spite of our anticipation, I was having a tough time staying focused. My thoughts kept flashing back to our cool, crystalline pool surrounded by thick, luxurious green foliage and the trickling waterfall. My mouth yearned for chilled champagne with bubbles dancing in a long-stemmed glass as I asked myself…"What in the HELL are we doing here?"

The odometer indicated we would soon reach the ranch. We had followed this dusty, dirt road for what seemed like a very long time. I too, like Sonny, had about 'had it'.

Ahead was a short incline, then a gradual drop into a magnificent valley. Suddenly, in the blink of an eye, the Wizard of Oz black-and-white to color-scenario came into view. One minute the land was dull and dim, the next bright and vibrant.

The boys and I saw this vision of striking green beauty. Around the perimeter stood white wooden fences, solidly lined with a kaleidoscope of roses. Lush irrigated pastures met the road and hearty cattle grazed beside a herd of wild deer.

A modern ranch house and an array of garages, one with a connecting cottage, came into view. Down the driveway a short distance away stood a modest dwelling. In anticipation I thought, "That must be our place."

Suddenly three ranch dogs charged up the road towards Lee, barking as though we were aliens. The cats who were with me instantly freaked and big dog Warbo was frantically trying to jump through the tiny windows of the V.W. bus.

We had arrived at our new home. It was the end of our lengthy journey.

A statuesque, elderly woman strolled from inside the ranch house towards us. She was wearing a yellow hard hat with gray curls peaking out, a blue sleeveless blouse, red pedal pushers and white canvas shoes. She approached us with a quick, confident gait with hands resting on slender hips. Motioning with strong gestures, she signaled us to go down a dirt roadway, where the small house I had noticed, stood.

We all piled out of our vehicles, delighting in the cool sprinkler mist blowing from the pasture. We inhaled the aroma of damp earth. What a welcome change from the choking dust that filled our nostrils during the long drive in.

As the woman walked up to greet us, she announced in a loud voice,

"Hello! I'm Della Mae Silbaugh. Welcome to my Rancho!"

The introduction between Mrs. S. and our family went smoothly. The meeting of our high-strung Great Dane and her mild-mannered Collie, Laddie, did not. Right away Warbo grabbed Laddie by the neck and flipped him into the air like a coin, catching him on the way down. The uninjured, timid Collie scurried off and crawled under a shed. Much to our relief, Mrs. S. commented, "That animal always has had low-self esteem." With that I recalled Judi telling us her Grandmother was a schoolteacher. She was no country bumpkin.

Mrs. Silbaugh was as anxious to show us our place as we were to see it. Her first comment as we stepped inside was, "There are no door keys to your house, they disappeared years ago." What an interesting comparison THAT was to what we had just left, a virtual fortress with alarms and gates in a city of crime.

The house showed its age, but was clean and smelled of fresh paint. The air-conditioner spread a refreshing chill throughout, giving us a cool, friendly greeting. A stove and refrigerator were in the kitchen and an adjoining, outside laundry room held a washer and dryer. A hallway off our bedroom had the same dimensions as the boy's bunk beds…with a foot to spare. The tour ended with a well- lit bathroom and walk-in storage closet.

At the rear of the house was a dry, rocky creek bed that Mrs. S. said, "Always brims full of water in the winter months and will overflow its banks and bring water close to the house." She was right, it did.

Four tree-lined reservoirs within easy walking distance, supplied the horses and cattle with drinking water. They were loaded with bass, and hundreds of croaking bull frogs gathered at the waters edge. Home was a virtual oasis! Home was a fisherman's paradise!

Mrs. S. outlined Lee's duties. He would start by moving irrigation pipes around in the two pastures every day. The cattle were pets and had to be taken there daily to graze.

"I have 81 cows, and calves, two bulls, and three horses. They all must be accounted for every morning. They'll have to be coaxed back out onto the range every evening with hay, just before dusk".

We Meet Ole Johnson

Ole and Dee Johnson

Part 3

WE MEET OLE JOHNSON

We'd been at the ranch two days when the pump on the well that supplied water to the houses quit working, meaning no water in the hottest part of the year. Lee checked the reset button with no luck. Mrs. S. confidently announced, "I'll call Mr. Johnson. He'll know what action to take." The name was familiar to us. Judi and Harvey had told us fascinating stories about this man who lived down the road from her grandmother.

Shortly, an old green pick-up truck came chugging in and stopped near the well where Lee waited. A man climbed down from the cab with a spirited, "Hello young fella. I'm Ole Johnson. I hear you're having trouble." Lee introduced himself and Ole got right down to business. Opening the relay box, he declared, "ANTS"!

"WHAT? ANTS!!" Lee exclaimed. Ole answered, "It's ants. They've moved into the box and made a nest in the points, which shorted out the connections."

He cleaned them all out, living and dead, turned on the power and the pump started right up. In the years to come, he would touch us deeply with his vast knowledge and love of nature.

Ole Johnson was a spry 60 year old man, five feet five inches tall, about 130 pounds. He had large ears and a wide flattened nose, where a pair of wire-rimmed glasses perched, magnifying his blue-gray eyes. His shoulders were hunched, causing his elbows to be held high, with the palms of his hands facing backward. He walked with a bowlegged gait. He always wore a denim shirt open at the throat, the sleeves rolled up above the elbow. To dress it up, he added a Bolo tie. Blue Wrangler jeans, and slip-on boots finished his attire. On top of it all, covering what there was of his thin, brown hair, his trademark Stetson, so unique that years later we've yet to see another like it. He called it a Shepherd's hat.

Ole had a deep, rich voice and he matched it with the vocabulary of a professor. He was a voracious reader and could speak eloquently on topics from science to philosophy. But first and foremost, his wisdom came from the Earth's school of hard knocks. This man on any given day might help deliver a set of triplet lambs and then an hour later, butcher a thousand pound steer.

He told mesmerizing stories to those who listened. He had the timing and presence of a stage actor. Often the subjects and story lines of his fables were hard to swallow, but later, you would hear talk of those same outrageous incidents, confirming their authenticity.

Ole was a husband, father, grandfather. A mentor, a leader of men, a teacher and a friend.

City Boy And The Rattlesnake

"Lee"

Part 4

CITY BOY AND THE RATTLESNAKES

✦ ✦

On the third day at the ranch, Mrs. Silbaugh's strict training of Do's and Don'ts began. The school teacher was about to start educating us. "There will be no alcohol or parties on this ranch." Now, Lee and I were far from heavy drinkers, but we did enjoy a beer around 4:30, which we deemed beer-thirty.

"No chickens, and as long as I live, no pigs on this property. Next year you can plant a vegetable garden behind my house so I can supervise it." Our dreams of having chickens and raising our own garden were shattered in three days and three short sentences. She went on, "Never yell or shout while herding the cattle. Speak softly and say 'Git' to make them go and sing out a melodious, 'Suey' to make them come to you." Neither of those terms worked for us. Flakes of hay in hand were the only way to budge those 83 head of cattle.

The incredible countryside surrounding us and our enthusiasm for a new life made it easier to cope with the rules. We learned a lot that first August. Lee became a fence builder, mechanic, handyman, veterinarian, gardener and...slayer of snakes!

Rattlesnakes were commonplace. They'd slither through the pastures, hide out in the barns and sun themselves in the sandy creekbeds. It was vital to watch where you walked.

The cats prowled nightly in search of them and when Spot found one, her paw resembled an inflated mitten from the swelling of the bite, but she recovered without a problem.

One evening the cats were romping in the yard near an overgrown honeysuckle vine. Suddenly we heard a distinct bzzz bzzz. They'd stirred up what sounded like a big one. Lee promptly yelled, "Bring the shotgun."

I ran inside, snatched up the gun with shells, delivered it to him and asked, "Lee, how are you going to see into that vine? It's too thick." Lee recalled something Ole had said a few weeks before, "When a rattler is in heavy underbrush and you can't see it, stick the barrel of the gun in and move it slowly back and forth to get the snake good and mad. Count to three and pull the trigger. The snake will line it's head up for you as it looks down the barrel of the gun." It worked. The intruder was dead.

The next week Lee was fixing a fence the cattle had mashed down. A swinging panel, in a gully five feet deep and ten feet wide had to be rebuilt. As he installed the new panel, concentrating on getting it level, he realized he was standing on what felt like a hose but the hose moved. He looked down to see a rattlesnake's head protruding out from underneath his boot where his big toe was and a two foot long body with three inches of rattles sticking out on the other side of his boot. With one mighty lunge, he leapt flat-footed from the gully up to safety. Lee was badly shaken by the time he arrived home and hollered, "Honey, bring me a beer and keep them coming."

What's that old saying? "Rules are made to be broken." Well when it came to drinking a bit on the Silbaugh ranch we did just that. Not much you see, just in times of severe stress or thirst.

Mrs. S. had the eyes of an eagle with a clear view of our house and everything we did and kept a very tight rein.

Party Lines And Pasted Teeth

"Jim & Tim: Pastures, Cows"

Part 5

PARTY LINES AND PASTED TEETH

September was here, which meant the boys would be starting a new school. Reed's Creek school was fourteen miles east of the ranch, eleven of it on the same dusty, dirt road we'd traveled in on that first day of our new life.

Classes were from first through eighth grade. 63 children were enrolled, all of whom had been born and raised in the area. To our surprise, a school bus would pick up and deliver the boys home every day. The time and personal attention the teachers devoted to each student was so unlike the overcrowded schools in Los Angeles. In addition to the fine teaching they received, Jim and Tim were also quickly learning the modest ways of the farm children and what they did for fun.

The first technique the boys mastered was how to eavesdrop into the telephone party lines without being detected. The instant Tim got off the bus after learning about this skill, he raced into the kitchen and began dismantling our telephone exclaiming, "Mom! I'll be able to hear what everybody's saying about everybody else when I unscrew this part of the phone where you talk into and maybe they'll say something about me." He was right. When you unscrewed the mouthpiece no background noise could be heard and you could be entertained for hours!

However, the party line system was a nuisance you learned to live with if you wanted any communication with the outside world. There were six families on our line and it became a real challenge to get a dial tone. When you did, you knew people would be listening to every word you said. I confess, I did my share of snooping.

One comical conversation I listened in on was the day Ma Briggs told Granny Eaton, "You know, cousin Pearl has been having bad troubles with her false teeth staying in her mouth so the darned fool mixed up some fast settin' glue and pasted her teeth to her gums. The glue is dried hard now and Pearl can't open her mouth. I don't know what we're gonna do."

I often wondered what did happen after that. I never heard another word about it, on the phone line or in person.

Our other indoor entertainment at the ranch was three channels on the television; when we could get them.

Lee, That Bird Is Illegal!

"*Tim and the Snow Goose*"

Part 6

LEE, THAT BIRDS ILLEGAL! WE CAN GO TO JAIL

Our first winter at the ranch was a far cry from the mild Los Angeles weather we were accustomed to. It was a record setting year with chilling winds, countless inches of driving rain, and intense lightening and thunder. But it was also the time of year rich ranchers transported their cattle in trucks from summer mountain ranges down to the valley floor.

The neighboring ranch was owned by a cowboy named Roy who had thousands of acres of summer and winter pasture around the Red Bluff area. As the cold weather set in, his animals were trucked to the property that surrounded us on three sides.

He had overpopulated his range, and by Christmas his cattle were out of native grass to feed on. Late one afternoon Roy rode his high-headed stallion down our dirt lane, his barking cow dogs trailing him. Roy dismounted, kicked at the dogs and made this offer, "Lee, I will pay you $100 a month to feed 60 bales (three tons) of hay to my cattle every day."

Lee took the job before giving any thought as to what Mrs. S. might say. She'd made it clear on a few occasions Roy was a no-good scoundrel, but we needed the extra money. Lee dreaded telling her, but thankfully all she said was, "Don't let it interfere with your work here."

Roy gave Lee the use of a beat-up four-wheel drive truck, with no top and a battered flat-bed trailer behind. When the boys helped, they'd whoop and holler as flakes of hay bounced off the heads of the hungry, mooing cattle following the truck. Lee fulfilled a childhood fantasy. He'd get drenched with rain and covered in mud daily. He was not getting scolded for getting filthy and he was getting paid for doing it! The washer and dryer got a real workout that winter.

When work was finished, Lee and the boys enjoyed hunting or fishing, always bringing home something. One conquest that had eluded them so far was a goose and they were anxious to get one.

Roy had 4000 acres that held six reservoirs with good hunting grounds. One dark, drizzly day he showed up claiming to have seen a bunch of snow geese fly into his closest reservoir.

Lee and the boys piled into Roy's Jeep, with shotguns in hand. Excitedly, Jim yelled back to me, "We'll be eating goose for supper Mom!" They would sneak up the steep, slick bank of the reservoir, Roy in the lead with Lee and the boys somewhat behind.

Silently raising over the bank, Roy straightened, flexed and fired. Blam! Blam! The water erupted as countless white birds took off for the sky. Floating on the water was one snow goose. After wading out in the icy water to retrieve it, Lee checked it over by looking at the size and wing span when suddenly Roy screamed out,

"Aw shit, it's a gawd damn swan." He had just killed a protected bird, making it illegal to shoot in California. Roy turned pale, grabbed the swan and warned, "We gotta ditch this thing fast."

Lee was taught as a young boy and had preached to his sons, "If you kill something, you had better eat it." With that Lee snatched the swan from Roy's grasp who yelled hysterically, "Lee, that bird's illegal! We can go to jail!"

Lee replied, "What's this we? I didn't kill it, you did! But, since it's dead anyway, we are going to take it home and we're going to eat it."

Lee and the boys plucked that unlawful bird for hours. When they finally finished we weighed it at ten pounds.

Its dark blue skin looked less than appetizing, but I prepared and placed it in a covered roasting pan figuring it would be ready to serve in two and a half hours or so. At the end of two hours I placed vegetables around the bird and set the table for dinner.

Four hours later, the mushy vegetables, and the salad were ready to eat… but not the swan. It was like trying to insert a fork into a football. The boys were famished so they ate the veggies and salad. I later served them a piece of the meat, but their young, sturdy teeth could not penetrate it. They looked like two puppies gnawing on rawhide. We all reluctantly settled for chicken soup…not the 'bird' we had hoped to be eating for dinner.

The carcass continued roasting in water throughout the night.

By morning it was still tough, but by this time I refused to give up and I boiled it three more hours. The dark stringy meat made perfect tacos. They were the finest we'd ever eaten.

Under the circumstances, I know we did the right thing. I have it on authority from a Fish and Game person that a swan can live 30 years. We figured that tough old bird had to be 31!

Eggs For A Sale

"Billy Jo's Place"

Part 7

EGGS FOR A SALE

The trek to town was tedious, but became the highlight of our week. We still enjoyed the ranch as the months continued to pass, but the job became less enchanting.

Sunday was Lee's day off and after chores, our family headed for town or parts unknown to explore. On one of those Sundays, we passed a sign advertising 'EGGS FOR A SALE.'

We came to a screeching halt, backed up and quickly maneuvered into a narrow dirt driveway. Mongrel dogs ran to the van, snarling and snapping at the tires. Kinky-tailed cats, three pigs and a couple of snotty-nosed kids roamed the yard. Lee beeped the horn. No reply. He beeped again; this time longer. Still no response. We were about to leave when onto the shabby porch stepped a pregnant, barefoot girl with unkempt, brown hair, deep blue eyes and sheer ivory skin. A toddler clung to her frayed housedress. She drawled, "Whatcha want?"

"We saw a sign out front. Do you have any eggs for sale?" I asked.

"No, but ah gots milks for a sale. Mah chickens laid their selves outta eggs."

We cautiously exited the van as she yelled for the dogs to get back. Kids of all ages, one portly pig, some of the cats and a bunch of scrawny chickens surrounded us in curiosity. We introduced ourselves and she said, "Mah name's Billy Jo. Would ya likes some cold milks?" We couldn't pass up an offer like that.

Entering the house behind her, we observed four old, beat up but functional refrigerators and two antiquated stoves with massive black kettles of milk simmering on top. Her method of pasteurization by heating the milk on the stoves appeared safe, so we sampled some of the rich, cold bottled milk. Cream was floating on the top half. It was pure ambrosia. We became steady customers.

Billy Jo told us that she'd married at the age of thirteen. Her husband Ted (who she called Daddy) was a 40 year old Red Bluff mechanic. She was living proof of that old saying "barefoot and pregnant."

One spring Sunday afternoon, when we went to get our weekly milk and egg supply, Billy Jo greeted us at the door wearing an up-to-date, spotless party dress. Her hair was curled and pulled up into ringlets and she was wearing shoes. How cute she looked.

We inquired, "Why are you all dressed up?" Her answer stopped us in our tracks. "Mae liver and Mae utris fell out onta the floor last night so ah wants to look good when they buries me."

It happened, shortly after giving birth to her sixth child, so as far as we could figure out, whatever fell out must have had something to do with that.

The last we heard, Billy Jo and the kids were doing fine, but husband Daddy had passed away.

Owls On Paper

Owls In Cage Made From Buffet

Owls In Their Tree

Oliver

"Stanley & Oliver"

Part 8

STANLEY AND OLIVER

The morning Jim and Tim found them, they were trembling under a tall oak tree. They'd fallen from a nest and the boys carefully transported them home. Their frail bodies consisted of fluffy down and sharp beaks, softened by round, sleepy eyes. We learned they were Great Horned Owls. We named them Stanley and Oliver. The baby birds were fed a mixture of water and baby cereal through an eye dropper every two hours. We all took turns around the clock.

Stanley and Oliver grew quickly and soon, the shoe box we made for them when they arrived was too small. An old china cabinet fronted with chicken wire served as a perfect pen. Our front room was their home.

As they matured, feeding time was cut to twice a day. Stanley and Oliver would sit on newspapers over the kitchen table and devour hand-held, cut-up pieces of fish, and drink water fortified with vitamins from the eye-dropper. The owls were quite awkward, but extremely bold. Having them join our family after the recent move from Metropolis was magical.

Once a day the front lawn became their kingdom and they were free to roam, but with supervision. The next step was learning to fly. The tree in the yard was a perfect launch pad. We would speak to them softly and set them on a sturdy branch. After some contemplation they'd flap their wings and do a free fall onto the cool grass below…much of the time, comically ungraceful.

Stanley and Oliver were on their own in no time, with the exception of food. We suspected they did their share of hunting, but every evening at dusk they'd fly down to their tree in the yard, and loudly pop their beaks together. You could not mistake the noise. It sounded like dice being shaken. We'd greet the owls, feed them the cut up fish, and when full, they would fly away into the night skies once again.

Stanley and Oliver were as dependant on us as we were on them. We loved those birds and the time came when we'd get concerned when they did not show up for dinner when we thought they should.

Worrying was needless. They'd always fly down to their tree and raise holy hell begging for food just before dark.

Early, on a Fall morning we awoke to a loud, frightful clattering sound outside our bedroom window. Looking out, we saw Oliver, perched on a wooden fence post near the cow's watering trough. His wings were standing upright and his feathers looked like quills. He was extremely agitated.

Lee and I ran outside and discovered the water-drenched body of Stanley. He had flown into a wire, then tumbled into the cattles trough and drowned.

What an unexpected, tragic event. Oliver and our family lost a cherished friend that day.

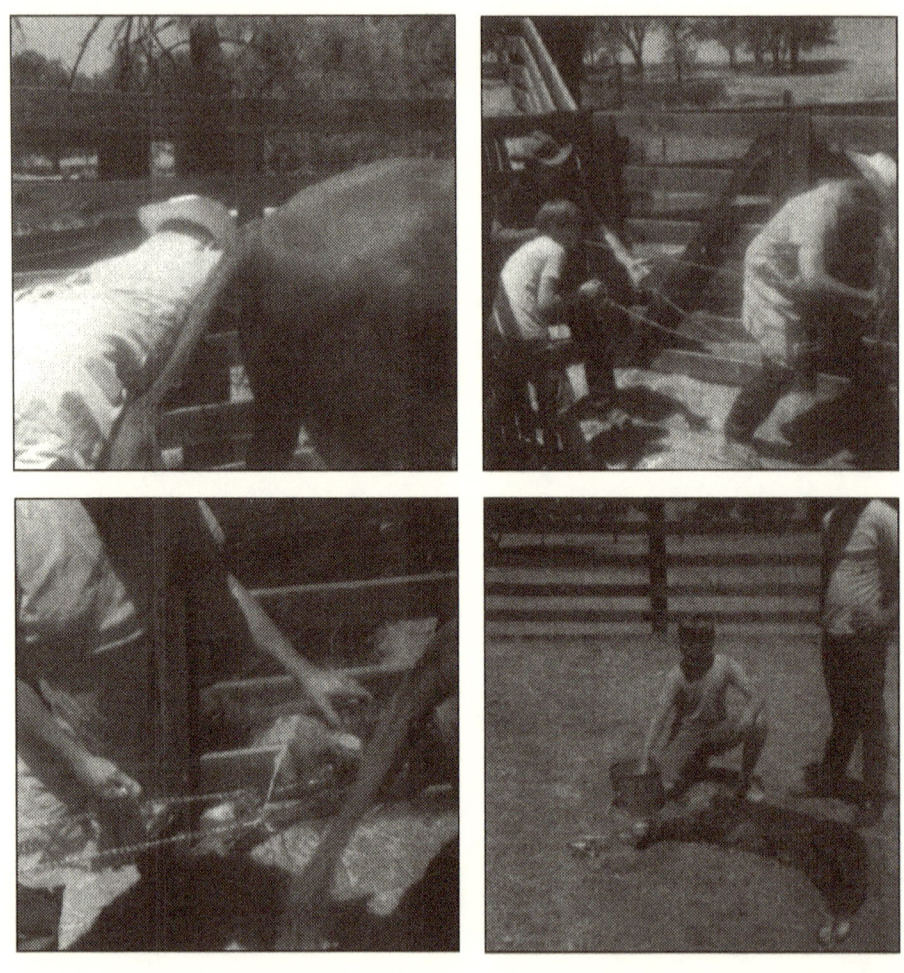

Lay-Lady-Lay And Zig-Zag

Dr. Giambroni, Lee, Jim and Tim assisting in the birth of a calf

Part 9

LAY-LADY-LAY AND ZIG-ZAG

Knowing very little about cattle, we found ourselves ignorant of everyday terms Mrs. S., Ole and cowboy Roy used. Examples: a cow is a mature female, while a heifer is a young cow who's never had a calf. A steer is a castrated bull calf primarily used for consumption. A Hereford is a breed of beef cattle. The 83 head at the ranch were Polled Herefords meaning they were born without horns, a very desirable trait.

Some cattle diseases have intriguing names. We learned 'red nose' applied not just to Rudolph. Black leg had nothing to do with the cattle's leg color and blue tongue did not infer the animal was either extremely cold or dead. These are all serious viruses the herd had to be vaccinated against.

There were times when unforeseen problems arose as the cows were birthing. Then, a veterinarian was called out to help. One of the most dramatic births Lee and the boys were involved with was when a calf was turned side-ways and stuck solid in the mother's uterus. Dr. Giambroni had to reach up into the cow's womb, all the way up to his armpit and turn the calf by hand. The mother was so fatigued by then from pushing and trying to expel the calf, she was of no help when it came time for the delivery. Chains had to be tied around the back legs of the calf and it was actually winched out by Lee and Tim. The cow and the calf both survived, but both required a course of antibiotics for many days.

It was a Sunday afternoon when Cowboy Roy rode over to the ranch and asked, "Do you want a pregnant mare? I'll trade her to you in place of your usual pay for feeding my cattle next month." A horse of our own sounded like fun, so we accepted his deal and became the not-so-proud owners of a white, nasty tempered, sway-backed mare with pink-colored eyes. Lee turned her out with Mrs. S's. horses, who roamed the range all winter.

Early March our mare, Lay-Lady-Lay, ventured into the corral with her new born, spindly-legged, wild-eyed buckskin colt. We yelled to the boys, "Hey you guys! Come here and look what Lady brought in." They ran from the house and tried approaching the pair, but by then Lady was as wild as the wind and the colt was too. We named him Zig-Zag.

The unruly horses did not blend in on the ranch so we sold them cheap. The man who bought them showed up with a pricey, double-horse trailer. Lee informed him, "These horses are going to be a real problem to load. Would you like some help?"

"Oh, hell no! I've been doing this for years, go on about your business."

So, Lee left to finish some chores. When he checked back an hour later, the man's horse trailer had been destroyed completely. Zig-Zag had kicked the wooden floor out and it was laying in cow manure in the dusty corral. The severely damaged back doors were hanging off their hinges. The man was furious, jumping up and down, flailing his arms about like a crazy person. He was cursing the horses and screaming in a high falsetto voice about having to borrow a horse trailer because the S.O.B.'n horses had screwed his up.

The hapless man returned the next day with two cowboys to help load Lady and Zig-Zag. The horse trailer had a metal floor.

We saw him later in the year and he lamented, "That fool colt never did gentle down. He broke his neck trying to jump a high corral fence."

Lay-Lady-Lay And Zig-Zag

"Horses"

Oliver

"*Oliver*"

Part 10

AFTER EIGHTEEN MONTHS IT WAS TIME TO MOVE ON

Spring brought roses, wildflowers, green grass, newborn calves, and ranch explorations. We commonly heard the boys say, "Let's take the motorcycle and bicycles and see what we can see." We found forgotten dumps holding rusty square nails, ancient bottles and colorful pottery. We spent hours probing and searching, uncovering mementoes from yesteryear. Treasures still resting, where they had been discarded a 100 years before.

A lot of the discoveries were made around abandoned home sights where twisted, dead wood fruit trees now stood as barren guardians over yellow poppies and vivid wildflowers. The wind whispered through knolls of towering oak trees and you could almost hear the voices and feel the presence of the pioneers who lived there so long ago.

That same spring of 1971 we lost our great dane Warbo. He'd suffered an injury to his shoulder a few months before after racing full speed into a barbed wire fence in pursuit of a fleeing jack rabbit. The vet told us, "Your dog has Osteomyelitis (bone cancer) brought on by that previous puncture wound and he's in considerable pain. I recommend you put him to sleep." We followed his advice and said goodbye to Warbo.

After eighteen months of the restrictive and confining situation at Mrs. S's ranch, we decided it was time to move on. Thankfully, she understood and soon hired another person to take over.

We will always be grateful to her for giving us two important things, a landing pad in our escape from the big city and a launching pad to further our dreams.

Milt, the school bus driver and ranch owner, would be the perfect person to let know we were looking for a new place. He knew everyone around and could keep his ears open. As luck would have it, Milt informed us, "I need someone like you to be caretakers on my 160 acre ranch. When do you want to move in?"

We met Milt and his wife Nancy at their ranch that same afternoon. The house had three bedrooms, and two bathrooms. A massive rock fireplace filled a wall in the front room. There was a barn the size of the Astrodome, some chicken coups, a corral, and reservoirs filled with fish. Nancy said, "This place is for sale but you can call it home until it sells." They wanted us to keep an eye on it and show it to any potential buyers.

Our place on Briggs road was ten miles east of Mrs.S's. ranch via dirt roads. During one of our moving trips, I glanced sideways out Bay Fever's window. "Lee!" I shouted. "Oliver is flying beside us!" Our owl decided his home was with us!

In the beginning he spent time going back and forth between ranches. He'd show up frequently and call to us from the trees. We didn't see or hear him for several weeks. Then, one early evening in May, Oliver and a mate flew in and perched on a tree for an hour or so. He clacked and popped his beak a few times and the owls flew off together. It was the last time we ever saw him.

I'm sure there are many Great Horned owls flying around Red Bluff that our Oliver and his mate parented. We often wonder if the wise old boy is still around? Could be...

Green Rooster & Purple Hen

"Lee in Division of Forestry Truck"

Part 11

A GREEN ROOSTER WAS IN PURSUIT OF A PURPLE HEN

S oon after moving, we bought three pregnant ewes (sheep) from Ole Johnson. Then added five geese, three roosters, fourteen chickens, one turkey named Sam, a pig called Arnold, and Zambini, a foul-smelling Billy goat. Add in there somewhere, Barney a St. Bernard puppy, and a young Labrador Retriever, Mary Lou.

All our animals were friendly, but not very useful. They insisted on hanging around the front and back porches. Every time we went outside, we always stepped in something. But it was heaven.

The reservoirs had fish and an over-abundance of frogs. Lee asked Ole, "How do we catch frogs?" He answered, "Get a gig at the hardware store. It's a sharp, three-pronged harpoon-type device that can be attached to a broomstick or pole."

We set Tim loose with the gig and within an hour he brought home several large frogs. I fried the legs in butter and wine, and they were very tasty.

After school, Tim would hop on his bike with the gig wired onto the frame and 'frog' until he had a sack full.

Out of necessity, I became creative with various ways to prepare them. We used cooked, cold frog meat in salads. I made frog chowder and even put creamed frog over toast. But our favorite turned out to be...frog taco's!

Our budget was tight without the $150.00 a month paycheck from Mrs. S., but we lived off the land so generous with game.

When the house in Los Angeles finally sold, it gave us a little over $200.00 a month. Instead of patronizing places like Bullock's and Broadway Department stores, as I had done in Los Angeles, I now shopped at Thrift shops and yard sales.

Lee was hired back briefly to work for Cowboy Roy. He got involved in branding, castrating, dehorning and inoculating. Dehorning was a bloody, brutal job he did not enjoy. When summer arrived, Roy's cattle were transported to his summer range and Lee's job was finished.

We were just hanging out at the ranch one afternoon when a Division of Forestry truck pulled in, checking for fire hazards. Lee struck up a conversation with the men and within ten minutes, they'd offered him a job. Their cook had retired and the men were taking turns cooking and none of them knew how. Lee boasted, "I'm a great cook. When can I start?"

The chief invited him over to the station to fill out forms and very soon after, he had an appointment in Sacramento to take physical, written and oral exams. He passed them easily and obtained the job. The fire station was nearby and the pay was good. The men enjoyed his cooking, so along with that and being the food purchaser, he received vast experience fighting fires.

There were no rules at the Briggs Road ranch on how many animals we could have. Ole gave us several bummer lambs, newborns whose mothers either had multiple births or died giving birth. We raised the abandoned babies by hand, making their formula from evaporated milk and water. Nipples stretched over filled glass coke bottles were their sustenance and security. The lambs would baa impatiently waiting for their turn to eat. Feeding time was frantic and it had to be every few hours.

We didn't have the heart to eat any of our lambs. They were tame and if you weren't quick at the door they'd race inside and spring up onto the vinyl sofa. A lamb we called Catastrophe, once jumped into the fireplace and singed his hoofs but suffered no permanent injury.

When we wanted to eat lamb, Ole would drive over and take one of our yearlings. A face we'd learned to love and who's name we'd never forget, would be exchanged for a lamb from his ranch that we had no emotional connections with. That's just the way it was.

On a clear, warm day in May, our Labrador, Mary Lou was having her first birthday celebration and a few of her doggy friends had dropped by the ranch. They were racing around the yard wearing tall, pointed party hats on their heads. They looked so colorful I came up with a brilliant idea. I would dye all of our white chickens with Easter egg dye. I gathered up empty feed buckets and filled them with water and food coloring. Then I quickly dipped each chicken into the assorted shades. The birds suffered no damage, they turned out extremely festive and you'd swear, they were proud of their fresh, new look, as they strode with confident steps, scratching the ground for bugs and worms.

Later that afternoon, a neighbor from a nearby ranch stopped by in search of some of his stray cattle. The man was a notoriously heavy drinker and that day was no exception. His eyes had a glazed look as he silently swayed in the non-existent breeze.

Just as he finished asking if we'd seen his cattle, two of the dyed chickens ran past him. A green rooster was in hot pursuit of a purple hen. The man babbled, "Whatsa matter wiz soze shickens?"

Lee replied, "What chickens?" Visibly shaken the man repeated his question. "You heard me, its soze shickens, whatsa matter wiz em?"

Lee didn't have the heart to lead him on any further and told him what I had done. The expression of relief on the man's face was a look we will never forget.

A week later he found his missing cattle and the dye had worn off the chickens. In thinking back, I feel certain it was best that he'd not encountered the dogs running around the ranch in their pointed party hats.

Mary Lou, Missy And Cin

"The Labradors in their Party Hats"

My Family Needs A Place

"The Morris Ranch, 1974"

My Family Needs A Place

◆━━━━━━━━━━━━━━━━━━━━━━━◆

"Lee's Ingenious Animal Hauler"

⸻ ✦ ⸻

Part 12

MY FAMILY NEEDS A PLACE TO LIVE

With all of the commuting on the pot-holed country roads, the yellow van simply wore out. Bay Fever was still operable, but with all of our livestock, we needed a pick-up truck. We sold it for a good price and bought a beat up old, unsightly but reliable, truck. For my driving pleasure we purchased a elderly Cadillac with low miles.

The Briggs Road ranch sold in 1973, so we had to find another house pronto. We weren't having a bit of luck until one day, in desperation, we took a drive east up a winding dirt road surrounded by long, flat rolling hills. Ultimately the road ended.

There, an antiquated house stood. It had obviously been vacant for years. We stepped inside through the splintered back door. The place was in chaos, but appeared to be sturdy. After numerous inquiries we located the owners, Mr. and Mrs. Morris. I telephoned and spoke with both of them.

I introduced myself and began, "My family needs a place to live. If we clean up your ranch house and make the necessary repairs, can we stay there rent free?" They questioned our sanity for wanting to inhabit the place, but said it would be ok. Their personal headquarters were five miles away, down another dirt road. It was a working cattle ranch on 6,000 acres.

The old house we were to refurbish and reside in, was on part of that ranch. It had been used for many years by traveling sheep shearer's, which accounted for its many rooms. They all required vast work and paint.

We had kept in touch with our friends in Los Angeles and when word got around we needed help fixing up an old house, they started arriving in droves. They all were ready to pitch in and work. Even Sonny, our hippie driver showed up. He'd heard somehow about our plight and thumbed a ride from Haight Ashbury in San Francisco to Red Bluff.

At that point, we still had to get the sheep and the other animals over to the Morris ranch. The old red pickup truck did not have high side rails so the animals could and would jump out of it during the move. Lee rigged up the most ingenious hauler ever known to modern man.

He found two old doors in the barn covered in some strange looking dried feces and put them up sideways on each side of the truck. Then he drilled holes in the doors and wired them to four upright, rusty metal stake posts that he welded to the inside of the bed of the truck. The tail-gate was too short, so he used a headboard from the kids bunk beds to fix that. It was all tied together with nylon string.

I was embarrassed to look at it. How uncivilized... It worked!

Red Bluff is a town of Country music, rodeos, wrangler jeans, and cowboys wearing Tony Lama boots who haul around bluish-spotted cow dogs in the back of their bumper-stickered pick-up trucks. Sometimes the dogs are black or red, but the boots remain the same. The cowboys are a rough and tough breed. They live and work on ranches usually handed down from generation to generation. Their roots always will be in Red Bluff.

The Iron Horse was a popular Saloon on Main Street with standing room only on the weekends. The hardwood dance floor was crammed with cowboys and cowgirls. They cuddled close, slowly swaying back and forth as a live western band played tear jerking, sorrowful songs. There was also a lot of do-si-do-ing and twirling of the girls in their full, frilly skirts by the cowboys in their black felt hats, with wads of chewing tobacco tucked in their cheeks or inside their lips. The Iron Horse was the "In Place" for the "In Crowd" – the night spot of choice in Red Bluff.

On Saturday night, our Los Angeles friends wanted some action after being stuck out at the ranch toiling away all week.

They were accustomed to the excitement and noise of the 'big city'.

We piled into three cars and set out for an evening at the Iron Horse Saloon. There were ten of us wanna-be hippies dressed in normal attire, but with love beads garnishing our necks. Sonny was the exception. He was a hippie through and through. Could Sonny possibly fit in at the Horse?

The lights were dim as we entered the Saloon. Our presence was accepted without problem as we peaceably merged with the cowboys. We were situated around a sizable table, drinking a few beers when suddenly the jukebox blared a 1970's Creedence Clearwater song, "Run through the Jungle." I immediately asked, "Where's Sonny?"

The crowded dance floor quickly emptied and we got a look at why everyone had retreated. It was Sonny. He was about to make a spectacle of himself. He appeared to be under some sort of spell. Gyrating, springing and twisting in mid-air, his unruly long hair and full-flowing beard seemed to propel his every move. His fringed leather vest, layers of beads and knee high moccasins were extremely out of place at the Iron Horse. He carried on and on and at some point changed the cavorting into a type of a ritualistic routine. His performance was truly astonishing, but then the song mercifully stopped and Sonny came to his senses.

Adjusting his head band, totally out of breath, he plopped down in a chair at our table. All eyes were on us. The locals were restless, but our area was swiftly surrounded by friends we'd made during our first years in Red Bluff, all highly regarded people of the community. The situation could have easily gotten out of hand.

The Sheriff had been notified and his deputies were visible in the Saloon, but were not called upon, as the situation had defused.

Last we heard of Sonny he had settled down, furthered his education and is now a respected Buddhist Monk.

Truly Content

"Arnold the Pig, Kissey Our Spotted Cow Dog
& Barney St Bernard"

Part 13

WE WERE TRULY CONTENT AT THE RANCH

D uring the two years we lived at the Briggs Road Ranch, we were involved in the Tehama County Fair. Lee's vegetable garden won the Sweepstakes award. My homemade jams, jellies, pickles, pies and photography won blue ribbons. Jim entered a lamb raised for his 4-H project and Tim showed two of his roosters. We all received ribbons for our efforts. We still cherish them.

Lee's Forestry job was seasonal, and the fire camp had closed for the winter. The renovations of our rent-free lodgings were now complete, and it was quite comfortable. But, the long road leading to the house had crater-like holes, making it impossible for the school bus to drive in. The boys had to be transported out each morning and picked up later in the day. There was one redeeming factor, however. After driving out to get them in the afternoon, we'd usually find our mailbox brimming with letters. Bills were few and far between. We owed no one and didn't have many. We were truly content at the ranch. Life was wonderful.

The foreman on the Morris ranch was their son, Mike, who ran a vast herd of beef cattle. One crisp fall afternoon Lee rode his motorcycle five miles to the Morris's headquarters and asked, "Do you have any work over here? I have experience with a lot of different ranch jobs." Mike answered, "We can always use a good hand. Come back tomorrow at dawn. We'll be rounding up cattle for branding."

The following day Lee became a regular employee on their ranch. Instead of a horse to ride, Lee was given a motorcycle for getting around the ranch. Right up his alley!

In early February 1975, two obvious high rollers came driving through the ranch in a new Lincoln Continental. The luxury car was a sight to see with its ornate gold-plated bull horns serving proudly as a gaudy hood ornament. The flashy plush seats were upholstered in leather hides from a brindle-hued bull.

The men were from Texas and had leased the Morris ranch with an option to buy. Within hours after their visit, truck load after truck load of Holstein cows, bulls and Mexican steers filled up the countryside. Only in movies had we seen anything to compare.

Within days, the profuse grasses on the surrounding hills were ravished from being overstocked with cattle and they were out of grass feed. With nothing left for the animals to eat, the Texans leased, with option to buy, yet another ranch from unsuspecting owners. In looking back, this must have come as a shock to the Morris's. Not only was their grass feed gone, but the lease would not be honored. We were out of the loop at that time and had no idea what the Texans were up to.

A week or so later, Lee was approached by one of the Texans, named Dallas, with a job proposal. The men had met Lee at the Morris's headquarters on numerous occasions and wanted him to move on with them to bigger and better things. He was offered a lucrative position with their Texas Cattle Company. The proposal they made was quite tempting.

Jim was attending classes and living at a dormitory at Shasta College in Redding. When the boys were born, my father set up a college fund for them which made that possible.

Tim had graduated from high school, so there was nothing tying us down. After some consideration, we decided to vacate our cozy home we had worked so hard to repair and follow the Texans. We relocated to Millville, California, a 45 minute drive north of Red Bluff. We were packed up and had the animals ready to resettle in one week's time.

Ranch House

Front Porch

Kitchen Before

Kitchen After

Front Room Before

Front Room After

"Next Stop Millville"

Part 14

NEXT STOP MILLVILLE

Our Millville dwelling stood in a magnificent valley lush with emerald green grasses. Sweet native berries were ripe for the picking and vivid wildflowers fluttered in the pristine air. The outmoded settler's home we were to occupy, was positioned just 60 feet from Cow Creek, where year-round, cascading waters flowed and salmon spawned in profusion. What a storybook setting.

We were moving into yet another vacant house in need of extensive clean-up, repair and paint. A shallow well on the property was impure so we could not drink the water. Lee hauled water from two miles away, which he drew from a natural spring.

The Texans had leased, with an option to buy, the lower ranch in Millville where we all lived. They resided with their families in two weathered homesteads on the opposite side of the ranch several miles away. Dallas and the other Texan, Buck, had also leased the upper ranch in Big Valley (Adin), owned by the same people whose kin had worked the land at both areas for generations.

The same people whose ancestor's graveyard occupies a lonely section of the lower ranch.

The two ranches had a combined total of 29,000 acres of fertile land and the Texans had complete control over it.

Shortly after arriving on Cow Creek, livestock trucks began bringing in the 2,000 head of cattle from the Morris ranch. They'd tied up the Morris property just long enough to devastate the land and generate enough cash from the cows real owners to fund the new venture at the Millville and Big Valley ranches. The way the Texans worked it, was to have contracts with several southern California cattle investors to pasture and take care of their animals. The payments they were supposed to pay the rancher who owned Millville and Big Valley grazing pastures, was just a drop in the bucket compared to revenue the cattle produced.

Thousands of dollars a month checks for board and care were sent from the cattle owners to Dallas and Buck. This money was in exchange for the Texas Cattle company's employees to purchase livestock, feed, to brand, inoculate and care for their bulls, cows, calves and steers. The out-of-the loop owners had never seen nor had any contact with their animals.

Laymen that we were in ranch management, and barely knowing Dallas and Buck, we were not aware of their fabrication of wealth.

On the surface, it appeared they could buy the entire state of California. The Texans had arrived and the northern part was about to take a bumpy ride.

They could break horses, sidestep bill collectors, make you believe the unbelievable, sweet talk anyone, charge anything they bought, seldom pay for anything they bought, misrepresent and usually not make payroll. Dallas and Buck donned western style clothes and gold chains befitting Pit-Bulls. They drank 100 proof whiskey, carried lengthy cigars-sometimes lit, sometimes not, and people liked them.

Lee was going to be a bona-fide cowboy so it was time to buy a pair of real cowboy boots. He'd always worn motorcycle boots but they would not be adequate for this job.

His primary assignment on Cow Creek was to look after and feed the cattle, keep fences in repair, irrigate the pastures and any other job needed doing. The ranches came stocked with horses of all types and temperaments. Lee selected his gelding from the vast selection at hand.

It was a thickset strawberry roan, understandably named Roanie.

The other cowboys snickered at Lee's choice. Roanie was far from the most attractive horse on the ranch with, eyes too small and close together for the size of his canoe-shaped head. But, in the months to follow Roanie proved to be a worthy stead.

It was hard to believe that five years had past since we left our handsome home, high on a hill, sold most of our worldly belongings, the business suits and well-shined shoes. We'd had so many adventures in those years, it all seemed so far away.

Next Stop Millville

"Lee and His Horse Roanie, Spring, 1976"

Send Your Pet Rock To Rockhaven

"*Tim and Calves*"

Part 15

SEND YOUR PET ROCK TO ROCKHAVEN RESORT

Dallas drove his Lincoln over to our side of the ranch in search of Lee just before daylight on Easter Sunday. Lee was out doing chores, so I invited him into the house. Without hesitation he drawled, "We'll be branging in some caves (calves) and will put'em in the pins over yonder. They'll be day old caves so yawl have to give'em milk in bottles."

When Lee came back for lunch, I told him about the calves that would be delivered. Tim was very anxious to have them at the ranch and was eagerly awaiting their arrival. Having a few calves underfoot would be a welcome change. The following afternoon three livestock trucks drove into the valley near the location where we obtained our drinking water.

Lee sent Tim home in the truck to get me. He hollered, "Mom, you have to come down to the corrals and see what's going on." It was a production to behold. The trucks had arrived with the calves. Dallas, Buck, Lee and three ranch hands from the upper ranch were unloading no less than 250 newborns.

The Texans had bought them from a local auction yard where the calves had been taken from their mothers sides shortly after birth, which is common practice. It brings the cow into her milk and she can then be utilized as a dairy animal. In such cases, her calf will typically sell to meat markets or restaurants who ready it for veal cutlet.

The lovable, day-old calves were unloaded and herded into a spacious barn with row after row of feeding troughs. The infants were motherless, frightened and famished. The scene was total chaos. First on the agenda, was to unpack case after case of one quart, heavy plastic feeding bottles with large pliable nipples attached. Next came the enormous responsibility of feeding all of those black and white, innocent-eyed babies.

After the calves ate, the emptied bottles and cartons of calf formula were transported by truck to our house. Mornings and afternoons, our kitchen became the hub of the calf operation. The formula was combined with hot tap water mixed in heavy metal pans. The bottles were filled, nipples attached and promptly delivered to the barn where each bottle was hung in individual wire bottle holders. The calves would hungrily strike the nipples from beneath with their moist, black noses trying to get milk to come down into their waiting mouths. They were watched closely during feeding time, more times than not they'd knock the bottle from the holder to the ground.

When the feeding frenzy was over, the bottles were removed from the hangers, cleaned, purified and delivered back to our kitchen, where they were readied for the next feeding that same afternoon.

After living at the ranch a few weeks, the calves put on weight and gained good strength. Combiotics were given the calves to protect them from invading viruses and pneumonia.

Then the unforeseeable happened. They started getting sick. The onset of scours (diarrhea) began. White muscle disease struck the herd and the majority of the calves could not be saved. It was a heart-wrenching experience to stand by and watch those sweet babies drop like flies. Ten percent lived to maturity. Just twenty-five of the 250 calves that arrived at the ranch survived.

Wanting something more to do and some additional income, I began breeding and selling Himalayan cats. The long haired kittens brought a hefty price. With tongue-in-cheek, I named my business The Cow Creek Cat House, which made for some raised eyebrows and chuckles. It required some attention, was fun and what were a few more animals around the place? But another venture had also caught my eye.

It was the early days of the Pet Rock craze and I founded a Pet Rock resort and advertised it in the National Enquirer. Seventeen Magazine picked up the story and Pet Rocks began arriving at the Millville Post Office. They came in all sizes, shapes and origins. Our favorite camper was Stoney. A gold colored five pounder with a leash, sent down from Canada. A list of specific instructions for his care was enclosed, along with his artfully decorated cardboard home.

The well-publicized Rockhaven Resort was the prime place to send your Pet Rock for ultimate rest and relaxation. A two week stay in the country, offered everything from Rock dances to Rockette-ball. After their 'adventures', the happy campers were shipped home to their anxious owners, complete with pictures, showing them proudly riding horseback and basking on the beach at Cow Creek. It was a fun and profitable project.

Big Valley, Adin, California

"Ranch House, Adin"

Part 16

BIG VALLEY, ADIN, CALIFORNIA

It was a Sunday morning in June when Dallas and Buck drove the Lincoln over to our side of the ranch. Chomping on a long cigar, Buck drawled, "Pack everythin' up, it's time to foller the cattle to summer range."

We had barely settled into yet another favorite house and didn't want to leave, but it would be north to Big Valley, Adin, California, a 100 mile journey to the high desert. For the first time ever, we had the luxury of a moving van and ranch workmen to help load us up for the move. We were off on another adventure.

Would we ever see our cherished Cow Creek home again?

Our lodging in Adin was an authentic ranch hand's house. The withered wallpaper with tan streaks from tobacco smoke and woodstove ash sitting thick on warped wooden floors showed it to be well seasoned with the memories of previous cowboys.

Missing plaster in wide ceiling gaps warned of a leaky roof. Monumental clean-up and repairs were required. The house stood isolated in the core of nowhere. At first sight, one might suspect it was dropped from the sky and simply landed there. It was vast, more spacious than the others we'd lived in. More space meant more scrubbing and painting.

Jim stayed behind to attend college, but Tim migrated with us to Adin, as did a few of our remaining animals...Barney, the St. Bernard, Kissy and Maxine, the cowdogs, and six quarrelsome cats.

All of our farm animals were gone by then, sold or given away.

Adin was a lonesome farming community with one general store. The natives were laid-back, friendly folk, born and raised around those parts, whose common topic of conversation was detailing a lynching of five outlaws by the Vigilantes in the nearby town of Lookout some 50 years prior.

Game was profuse in Adin. Many a morning I would load up a rifle and shoot our dinner. Anything in season that ventured into the front or back fields became the evening meal. Pheasant, sage hen and grouse were abundant.

Lee was either cowboying or hanging out with other ranch hands at local saloons. Tim found the place dull, so he moved back down to Redding, enrolled in Shasta College and lived in the dorm with his brother, Jim.

This left me alone a lot of the time. My high point every day was to cram the three eager-to-go-anywhere dogs into my recently acquired 1961 VW Bug. I packed a bottle of wine, a camera, a rifle and a shovel for our daily trek into the forsaken, but fascinating, desert. Searching the unexplored territory for anything old or unique made the solitary time go by quicker. On occasion, Lee would explore the land with us and sharing the time made it special.

Lee and two cowboys, Jimmy Harrison and Dakota Way (Kody) had been riding hard on the range gathering cattle. At seventeen years of age Jimmy had already developed into a journeyman cowboy. Kody was forty, flashy and a choice hand as well.

One nippy winter day the three of them witnessed a once-in-a lifetime occurrence. A Bald Eagle knocked a goose from the sky. Two other eagles kept its attention as the third swooped down like a dive bomber and hit it square. The goose fluttered its wings, lost altitude and crashed landed close to Kody. The eagles followed the goose to the ground in hopes of claiming their prey. But Kody scared the eagles off, took the goose and stuffed it in his saddlebag. Lee gave him some disapproving dialogue, but let the subject drop.

Kody carried the dead goose around in his saddlebag the rest of the afternoon. After herding the cattle to the designated corrals, they sent Jimmy with the horses back to headquarters.

Lee, Kody and the goose headed for a bar in the nearby town of Lookout.

After consuming whiskey to their fill, they teetered out to one of the Texan's ranch vehicles, a Toyota Land cruiser. Lee insisted on driving, almost colliding with the bar as they left.

The road from there led directly to our ranch house where I waited with supper, past ready to serve. Jimmy had arrived, but no Lee and no Kody. As the two wayward men wove down the highway heading for home, Kody rolled down the Land cruiser's window and threw something out. Lee asked, "What the hell are you doing Kody?"

Kody slurred "Thet takes care ah thet." Lee growled, "What did you do?" Kody's response was, "I threw the goose away, it weren't any good with the guts in it all day."

That enraged Lee." If you wanted it bad enough to steal it from the eagles you should eat the goose. Anyone that would do a dirty trick like that wouldn't take the time to wipe."

That got Kody's attention. Lee turned off of the lonely highway one mile from our house and ordered Kody to get out and walk back and get the goose. "No!" snapped Kody. Lee insisted "Go back and get it." "No, you wantta do something about it?" Kody snarled.

The fight was on. They squared off. Lee landed on his back in the middle of the road with his head hurting. Getting up off the ground he thought, 'be careful this guy is quick'. Bam! Lee was down again looking up at the stars. Infuriated, he sprung up and got a hold of Kody's finger and snapped it. As they rolled around scuffling in the dirt, Lee broke another one of Kody's fingers.

"You're crazy!" Kody gasped as he took off on foot heading in the direction of a swamp filled with quicksand and a five mile walk from his home. This left Lee standing in the road screaming, "Kody get back here. Come back." Kody kept going, fleeing in a full trot.

He stepped through a fence running parallel to the road into another field, most likely feeling a bit safer from Lee's wrath.

Lee could see him in the headlights but Kody was disappearing fast, which made him angrier. He jumped into the Toyota, put the headlights on high beam and for some reason, in his tipsy condition, decided he must get Kody back at all costs. He put the Toyota in low gear, drove through the barb wire fence, started accelerating, hit a second fence, floored it going through yet another to reach the field imprisoning his alleged escapee.

Kody knew he was in serious trouble with Lee barreling down on him. There were no trees or rocks for Kody to get behind. Some random sagebrush and a woodpecker-holed telegraph pole the diameter of a coffee can offered little help for the 200 pound man.

Ducking in back of the pole, Kody attempted to make himself appear as narrow as possible.

Lee continued accelerating. He hit around 50 mph, coming so close to the pole that he tore the Toyota's mirror off. He spun the vehicle around and aimed the headlights at the terrified Kody, who quickly rotated around to the back of the pole. Lee drove closer.

Kody took three steps away in an attempt to escape. Lee made a second pass at the pole, giving the man hardly enough time to jump back and peer out from behind it. Kody looked like a deer frozen in the headlights. Lee slid the car sideways, stopped in a cloud of dust and screamed, "Now you bullheaded S.O.B. Are you going to get in here or what?" Kody got in.

The two men momentarily stared at one another, then burst into tears. Reality had set in. It dawned on them how dangerous their dispute had become once they'd left the Lookout Bar.

Lee drove back out through the torn down fences, over the splintered fence posts and headed for home.

Jimmy and I had eaten and he'd gone back to his place. I was keeping dinner warm and was becoming concerned about Lee's whereabouts.

Finally, Lee and Kody barged through the front door, arm in arm, singing some sad off-keyed cowboy song. It was obvious to me they had been crying. Both men staggered to the dinner table, collapsed in their chairs and began shoveling in the food.

Periodically one would sigh and the other one sniffle.

By the time they'd finished eating, both men were getting a grip on the situation and started facing the facts of the mass destruction to the gates, cedar posts and surrounding fences.

As Kody left in the smashed up Toyota, they made plans for the following morning's repair jobs.

They met early at the crime scene. Kody arrived with his fingers in a homemade splint, fence fixing tools, wire and wood.

Lee took a hammer in case Kody was the vengeful type. Neither man said much that day. Maybe they were too hung over or just embarrassed. They have not discussed it since.

Big Valley, Adin, California

"*Lee and Jimmy Harrison Cowboy*"

Floyd & Myrtle Potts

"*Floyd & Myrtle Potts' House*"

Part 17

FLOYD AND MYRTLE POTTS

Floyd and Myrtle lived on the ranch many years before the Texans acquired it. They were the ones, in fact, who showed them the boundary lines. The Texans allowed the Potts to remain living in their old, run-down house if they watched for poachers, rustlers, trespassers and anything out of the ordinary.

Floyd and Myrtle were in their early 60's and definitely 'Deliverance' movie material. Floyd had wispy, muddy-colored hair styled in a bowl cut and a white, unruly mustache that called attention to his elongated, snaggled teeth. Winter or summer would find him wearing layers of tattered long-johns with bib overalls, which stopped several inches short of his black rubber goulashes.

Myrtle, nickname Myrt, was a woman of mountainous size. Waist-length, yellow-gray hair was pulled straight back and held in place by a strand of yarn. Her array of once colorful house dresses were threadbare with the fabric covering her bosom threatening to explode any moment.

By late 1975, the Texans were in financial difficulty and were attempting to generate cash flow above and beyond the revenue from cattle and hay sales. They came up with the idea of utilizing part of the ranch as an exclusive hunting club.

Deer were very abundant on the entire ranch, but they determined the thousands of acres that Floyd and Myrtle Potts lived on would be the best place for the project.

The Texans ran advertisements in newspapers, hunting magazines and had brochures printed with exaggerated claims. There was vigorous response to the costly club membership from doctors, lawyers and other professionals from all over California.

Two noted San Francisco sports journalists arrived one day. The Texans had offered them free hunting privileges in exchange for favorable publicity. Lee arranged to meet the journalists, Brian and Rusty, at ranch headquarters. There was plenty of room to spend the night, but the men opted to have Lee show them the area where the next morning hunt would take place.

Lee drove his jeep and they followed him, in their magnificent motor home, some ten miles east to the Potts farm. The short road in was uniquely fenced with car parts, disabled tractors, rusty water heaters, bed springs, rope and tangled wire. Chickens made their nests in sun-cracked tires in the front yard of the Pott's, old house.

Lee reached into his ice chest and pulled out three cold beers. Shortly, Myrtle burst from the house in all her splendor, waving wildly to show them where to park the motor home for the night. Lee introduced the apprehensive Brian and Rusty to her.

"Mah husban' Floyd'll be taken ya out for the hunt in the mornin'. Don't worry 'bout breakest. Yawl be eatin' at our place. I'll wake ya when it's time".

Morning came all too soon with Myrt beating on the side of the motor home with a wooden spoon yelling, "Rise and shine. "Breakest in ten minutes."

With too much beer, too little supper and not enough sleep, the city dudes stumbled over to the Potts place. Floyd greeted them at the back porch, spitting out tobacco juice and a "Howdy" in the same breath. With an "Ain't this nice," as he kicked a path through dried dog and cat turds, allowing them to walk inside. The welcome aroma of strong coffee filled the kitchen as they were told to sit at a large hardwood table. One chair, a stool and three assorted-size boxes were situated around the table. Floyd immediately took the chair. Myrt served the coffee in stout brown mugs of World War II vintage. The table was set with plates and forks, no knives or spoons. Napkins tailored from discarded flour sacks finished the rag-tag table setting. Four big dogs quickly occupied the space underneath the table. Three black iron skillets bubbled on the massive wood stove.

Anxious to eat and get on with the morning hunt, the guys were delighted when Myrt presented them with piping hot biscuits from the oven. She plopped down the iron skillets at various points around the table, each one brimming with pork chops floating in two to three inches of grease. Floyd dug in eagerly. Brian and Rusty looked for their non-existent knifes and then at one another, wondering how they were supposed to eat the greasy chops. Myrt bellowed, "Don't be shy boys. Dig in. There's plinty for both ya."

In a flash, Floyd and Myrt had their plates full and were dipping biscuits into the skillets with scooping motions, grease trailing from the pans to their mouths. With nothing to do but proceed, the guys began eating. Floyd had gnawed the chops down to the bones and without a single downward glance or change in conversation, he dropped the remains under the table. A dog fight broke out immediately. The growling, snapping dogs bumped and bashed the table, sending hot coffee splashing and puddling to the floor. It was bedlam at the breakfast table.

Lee met up with Brian and Rusty shortly before their return home to San Francisco. According to them, it was eight A.M. when Floyd finally got on with the deer hunt. The guys were thrilled and both came back with major-sized bucks. They quickly related to Lee on how the hunt went, but went on and on chattering non-stop about the breakfast served in the Pott's kitchen.

"*Lee, Jeannine & Outhouse on Cow Creek, 1976*"

Part 18

IT WAS A RACE AGAINST TIME

I t was early December, 1976. Winter was clearly upon us with freezing temperatures, sleet and snow. Long past time for the cattle to be relocated back down from Adin to the Millville ranch.

Rounding up the cattle for the move was a major endeavor.

The Texans, the cowboys, other ranch hands, and the animals had returned to the lower ranch, leaving Lee and myself in Adin another two weeks to tie up loose ends and make certain no cattle remained out on the range.

Lee's Adin job was over and we were more than a little anxious to be returning to our Cow Creek home. We rented a sizable U-Haul truck, but it was questionable whether it could make it through the snowdrifts on the road into our place. The move became a race against time. We had to pack the truck with cartons of belongings and furniture, before a predicted blizzard hit. It was snowing, the wind chill factor sixteen below zero, making the furniture seem much heavier. We managed to get loaded without serious injury to ourselves and headed home.

Six days before Christmas our vacant Millville house had bare floors, vacant walls and empty cupboards. We quickly transformed it into our cozy, familiar surroundings. We selected a magnificent tree from a nearby knoll. The freezer held a turkey in readiness for Christmas day. Jim and Tim would join us for the holidays. We had returned to our beloved Cow Creek quarters.

Dallas and Buck were in serious financial trouble by then and paychecks were few and far between. Perhaps we should have anticipated what came next.

Three days before Christmas, a County Marshal served us with eviction papers. Unbeknownst to us, the Texans had not made any of the payments on our Cow Creek house that had been part of the original deal.

We had no choice but to pack up and leave. We ended up in a medicine shed used for storing antibiotics, salt licks and saddles. It was near the spring where Lee hauled our fresh drinking water to our now vacated house, and close to the barn where the bottle fed calves had died many months before.

The Marshal returned the afternoon of Christmas Eve to lock the house down and make certain we were leaving. Feeling bad about the situation and being in the Christmas spirit, he helped transfer our box spring and mattress to the cement floor of the shed. The remainder of our personal belongings went into a horse stall.

Our new home was a 10 by 12 foot structure, had no running water or bathroom facilities. But there was electricity. A battered refrigerator containing cattle medications provided us with some space for food. A weathered, one hole outhouse likely built in the 1940's stood several yards away.

We had abandoned our freshly cut, festively trimmed Christmas tree. There was no room for it now. A lone tree branch with mistletoe sprigs became our symbol of the holidays in 1976. Lee's job as ranch foreman was no longer a viable option. The Texans had lost their contacts and were being sued by the cattle owners, as well as local merchants and veterinarians around the Redding area.

The weather was wet and windy during the weeks we lived in the medicine shed. We spent long hours playing our modest stereo with the volume turned high. One lyric routinely blasted through the speakers, truly befitting the setting. "Rain drops keep falling on my head."

Often times the music was hushed by the clap of thunder and the racket of falling rain, as it cascaded down on the galvanized metal roof. We spent the evenings sprawled on our mattress with the three dogs, drinking cheap wine and recalling our adventures and misadventures, and wondering what our next move would be.

Race Against Time

"*Lee, Jeannine Looking out of Medicine Shed*"

Closed In On All Sides

"*Lee and D-8 Cat*"

Part 19

WE WERE CLOSED IN ON ALL SIDES

It was bitter cold as I washed my hair in the winter water from the corral hose. Just as I finished, Dallas drove up and announced they'd found a proper place for us to live and had another job proposition for Lee with their freshly formed Texas Lumber Company.

Bella Vista was our next stop, just a half hour drive northwest of Cow Creek. It was a small town with a Post Office, one gas station, a market and three bars. Bella Vista was a mere fifteen minute drive to the sizable city of Redding.

Our new residence was a new, double-wide mobile home sitting on a scanty, level lot closed in on all sides by neighbors.

We were fenced in. The paved streets and cement driveway were very foreign to us by that time. Quite a radical change from the freedom of the thousands of acres we'd lived on for the past eight years.

The lumber operation was the Texan's latest scheme to cause chaos on Cow Creek. The prior lush green fields were now barren and weed infested. The pastures, devoid of any livestock. They had destroyed all but the towering trees and the trees were soon destined to go.

Nearby ranchers were up-in-arms as they watched the ravaged trees being shipped by truckloads from the valley floor. Tension and malice were growing quickly between the locals and the Texans.

Lee's job was not to fall the trees, but to drag the logs to a landing site with a D8 Cat. Timber cutting continued through most of June of 1977.

Lee would track the Texans down periodically and they'd provide him with a pittance of money or a package or two of frozen beef. He had not been paid a full wage for months and decided it was time to quit working for Dallas and Buck.

About a month later, we heard Buck had been put in jail. I instantly drove to the market and bought a newspaper. The headlines read 'Businessman arrested on POT cultivation charge'. The article continued with, 'An acre of marijuana plants growing off South Cow Creek was discovered by Shasta County sheriffs agents.' They had booked Buck, but he was later released on $2,000.00 bail.

The agent said the acre had one plant every 18 inches, and the crop would have yielded an estimated $650,000 had it hit the market. A warrant had also been obtained for Benny, the ranch pilot. Buck was never convicted of the marijuana cultivation charge and Benny never resurfaced. Dallas returned to Texas where his wife divorced him.

We had the $233.00 a month payment coming in from the sale of the Los Angeles house, but it was definitely not enough to live on. The monthly rent on the new mobile home the Texans were paying for cost double that. So we moved again, into a older, smaller mobile home a block away.

Lee began frequenting the service station in Bella Vista and before long, the owner, Bruce, made him a job offer pumping gas. It was steady work, close to home and Fridays we could count on a paycheck. The job soon expanded and Lee began driving Bruce's tow truck, where he handled a lot of business for the C.H.P. (California Highway Patrol).

Most afternoons at the gas station were slow, so fishing with Bruce at nearby Shasta Lake became a regular thing for Lee.

Bruce and Mary had a mobile home on one acre which they offered to rent to us. We packed up and moved once again, two blocks away.

Mary's lifetime dream was to own a restaurant and the dream became a reality in 1980. A mini-mart and café were added onto Bruce's gas station and I began working with her, cooking and waitressing at the 'Whatever' Cafe. Mary and I were both home style cooks, and prepared food from scratch. Patrons grew steadily, tips were sizeable and Lee and I both had work we totally enjoyed.

Life was good again.

In my spare time I made extra money with a recycled idea left over from the Pet Rock resort over on Cow Creek. Instead of 'Rockhaven Resort', new services were offered to the owners of elderly Pet rocks at, 'Resthaven Cemetery'. After an article and pictures appeared in the Redding newspaper we received many deceased rocks. Some had actually visited the camp on Cow Creek years before.

Bruce and Mary's son and wife needed a place to live so we moved out, so they could move in. Would this shuffling from town to town, home to home ever end?

This time we rented a true trailer. The type you could tow behind a truck. It was a faded aqua blue, 1959 aluminum beauty that sat on its axels in a bed of sand. It was located in Jones Valley near Lake Shasta, six miles north of Bella Vista and rented for $165.00 a month. Barney, our loveable St. Bernard had died of old age. Maxine the cow dog, who once barked thunderously when a car entered her area, now lie unaware in the middle of the driveway. She was deaf and had dogzheimer's. We'd have to stop the car, get out and help her hobble off to the side.

Someone thought we should have an active dog so we were given a six week old Fox Terrier, beagle cross pup. We named her Bella Vista. Bell for short.

Hell Yes!

---◆--------------------------------◆---

"Patty Willis, Aviatrix"

Part 20

"HELL YES! I LANDED A DAMN PLANE THERE."

In April, 1984 Lee's mother Patty fell and shattered her right shoulder and left knee. She lived alone in Los Angeles and desperately needed her only child's help. We arrived the following day in the city we'd abandoned fifteen years prior. Lee and I didn't know quite what to expect, returning to the place we had dubbed the 'City of Crime', but it didn't appear any worse off than it was the day we left.

Patty was hospitalized four weeks, during which time doctor's detected serious cancers throughout her body. The prognosis was poor. Physical therapy and radiation began. We took a quick trip home to Jones Valley, quit our jobs, packed a few belongings and notified the landlady we'd be gone for an indefinite period of time. We did continue renting the old aqua-blue trailer. When this current concern was resolved we would still need a place to call home.

For the first six months we lived in the family house with Patty and her dogs, as well as our three dogs. She now lay terminally ill, in the exact same bed her aged mother had occupied. Patty had put her own life on hold to care for her Mom until she passed, a few years earlier. The situation was extremely stressful for all of us and a plan for privacy began.

We renovated a one room storehouse on the property, used as a catch-all. Patty financed the project and gave us money to live on every month. Having our own space was better, but every so often, the confinement of the 20 by 20 room would get to be too much and we'd make a bee-line home, 600 miles north to our faded blue trailer that sat in the sand near Lake Shasta.

We'd stay there a day or two, re-group, then return to Patty, the doctor's, the hospitals and the stress.

The house Patty and her mother had lived in, was built in 1929 by Lee's grandfather. Behind what we called, our playhouse home, was a grand old mansion that had been moved onto the property from Beverly Hills in the 1930's. Patty used it as a rental for income but Lee's great-grandparents had lived there when he was a child.

The feeling of family was everywhere.

We were five minutes from the heart of downtown Los Angeles, yet the spot on the hill was serene and a world away from the hustle and hassle of the city. Squirrels scampered from limb to limb in a pecan tree far above the rock patio that Papa had made and birds gathered findings for springtime nests. It was inspiring.

Lee's Mother was a free spirit from way back. She'd obtained a flying license at age nineteen and was a popular woman pilot in the 1920's. Lee had grown up around her friends, Amelia Earhart, Pancho Barnes and other pioneer flyers. At age 74, Patty Willis still had a lot of spirit and spunk.

After her broken shoulder was surgically repaired, her Korean surgeon informed her she would have to go to a physical rehabilitation doctor. She didn't like him or his foreign accent.

The rehab office was located on Pico Blvd. and the surgeon asked her, "Potty, do you know where PEE-KO Boulevard is?"

This insulted her and she yelled back, "Hell yes I do! I landed a damn airplane on PEE-KO Boulevard, so I think I can find it with my car."

Near the end of her life, Lee asked inquisitively, "Mom, do you think you could still fly an airplane? Get it up and get it down safely?" Her immediate answer was, "Hell yes! And I can fly the crate it was shipped in too!"

Lee's Mother passed away August 1st, 1985, sixteen months after her fall. It was time for tremendous soul-searching in dealing with the family homes. Lee did not want to sell them and since the other home was already being rented, that's what we decided to do with Patty's house.

There was unimaginable work ahead. The families collection of memorabilia and various articles and treasures occupied three garages, two attics and the basements of both houses. We eventually got most everything moved up north. No moving van. Just the two of us driving--back and forth--back and forth.

No sooner had life become (we thought), under control, than the tenants called and said, "The house had been burglarized!" The intruders had shattered windows and destroyed doors. We returned to Los Angeles. Being landlords, 600 miles away was not working out and the rents were always late. Finally, after months of anguish, we sold the houses and put them behind us, once and for all.

There was an amazing, almost overwhelming, amount of family possessions to go through and sort. It soon became apparent folks living in the old days did not throw much away. We found oddities like carefully wrapped turkey bones labeled, Thanksgiving '1898.' There were marked packages of neatly preserved tinsel from Christmas '1909.' The chore was emotionally difficult. When we'd come across a part of the past, like the bones and the tinsel, it would conjure up memories for Lee of his close knit family. It flowed forth into our lives and filled our space with sadness. We kept a lot of the family possessions but had to liquidate the rest through estate and yard sales. We moved to a larger and nicer rental three blocks away from the old blue trailer.

We began investing funds from the sale of the family homes in mobile homes in Jones Valley, near Lake Shasta. The following year we bought the rental we'd been living in and still reside in it.

The faded aqua blue trailer with the axles in the sand and the mobile next door to it went up for sale. Of course, we bought them both. There will always be a soft spot in our hearts for that special, old tin trailer. It is no longer blue, and has had major improvements made. Our son Tim lives there now.

Thirty five years have past since we sold the Business Suits and bought the Cowboy Boots. We arrived at the Silbaugh ranch in 1969 with confidence and expectations surpassing description.

We took a gigantic leap of faith and there has never been a single regret for leaving our flashy home in the city or Lee's prestigious job.

If we'd stayed in Los Angeles, our lives would never have been touched so deeply by Ole Johnson, our owls, Stanley and Oliver, the farm animals, the Pott's and yes, even the damn Texans.

We shared so much fun with our sons, all of us together, learning the ropes on the ranches. Our everyday adventures, the ups, the downs, misadventures, unexpected experiences, the happy and the not so happy times were worth more than all of the worlds' riches.

Lee's job was complex, challenging and a lot of hard work. He was part ranch-hand and engineer, part doctor and philosopher.

That city kid turned out to be one helluva cowboy.

If the telephone rang today and the opportunity arose for another adventure, I'd want to leave our present home in search of the unknown. I yearn to have chickens, some precious lambs, a pig, and maybe even a smelly old Billy goat. I actually miss going out on the porch and not stepping in something.

It is my strong recommendation, if anyone ever gives you the chance to give up the Suits and put on the Boots...by all means...GO FOR IT!

Our Play House

The Important Things In Life – 3 Dogs, Mattress, Sleeping Bag, Radio & TP

"Hell Yes!"

Part 21

WHATEVER HAPPENED TO??

Dr. and Mrs. Harvey Freed
Harvey is a periodontist in Southern California
Judi is the office Manager

Della Mae Silbaugh
Died at the ranch in 1973

Cowboy Roy
Died in 1980

Ole and Dee Johnson
Ole died in 1983, Dee in 1985

Milt and Nancy Nichols
Ranch owners, Red Bluff

Sonny the Hippy
Now Reverend Sonlon Kay, Buddhist Monk

The Morris family
Ranchers, Red Bluff

Dallas
Bankrupt in New Mexico, transports himself to bars on a riding lawn mower

Buck
Buys and sells used cars in Oklahoma

Jimmy Harrison
Family man and working Cowboy in Bella Vista, Calif.

Kody Way
Ranch owner

Floyd and Myrtle Potts
Both alive and residing in an assisted living facility

Bruce and Mary Emmons
Retired service station and café owners in Bella Vista

Patty Willis Seely
Lee's Mom, renowned woman pilot of the 1920's, died August, 1985

Jim (Fox)
Our 48 year old son; single family man, works at The Carpet Mart in Redding, Calif.

Tim
Our 47 year old son; single, works for Progressive Drywall in Redding, Calif.

Lee
The guy who shed the Suits for the Boots. Now 69 years old. Keeps in shape by riding motorcycles in the dirt, golfing, and mountain biking

Jeannine (Me)
67, manager of our rentals in Jones Valley, yard sale junkie, Senior Fitness Instructor and power seller on Ebay

'Roanie'
Lee's horse the strawberry roan, was bought after the ranch sold and went on to become a pick-up pony for a famous rodeo

'Beau'
Tim's horse, was sold to a young cowgirl. The girl and Beau won the National championship in Barrel racing

Our old aqua blue trailer with its axels in the sand burned to the ground in the Bear Fire, Jones Valley 8-11-04.

www.ingramcontent.com/pod-product-compliance
Lightning Source LLC
Chambersburg PA
CBHW030401290526
45785CB00004B/1859